A Text Book of

Fundamentals of Banking and Insurance-Part I

FOR BBA & BBA (IB)

(As Per Syllabus of New Education Policy)

Surjeet Kumar

(DR. P . A. Inamdar University)

Fundamentals
of
Banking and Insurance -Part-I

Asst. Prof. Surjeet Kumar

(B. Com. M. Com., MH-SET, TS-SET, PGDIBO, Completed PCC Examination of CA.)

Also Useful for

1. Along with BBA and BBA(IB) this book is useful for Certificate, Diploma and Undergraduate courses offered by various state and central universities.

2. A complete Textbook for everyone interested in learning about Banking and Insurance.

3. This book is worth reading for academicians, researchers, and corporate leaders as well.

License Notes

Disclaimer:-

"We've packed this book with the latest financial insights, along with some history thrown in for good measure! Of course, no book is perfect. If you spot something amiss, drop us a line! We'd love to hear from you and keep this book top-notch for future readers."

e-mail: hmrspoetry@gmail.com

Dedicated to

Maa Saraswati

Acknowledgement

First and foremost, I express my gratitude to the Supreme God, who inspires me to write with ease and creativity. I cannot imagine the completion of this book without the blessings of my parents, support of wife and cooperation of Ajit. I express my gratitude to all my teachers, students, friends, well-wishers, and critics whose feedback provides me with subjects to write about even more. How can I forget to express my gratitude to my readers and students, whose suggestions act as fuel for my writing.

Index

Chapter 01

Introduction and History of Banks

1.1. Definitions of Banks

A bank is a financial institution licensed to receive deposits and make loans. Banks may also provide financial services such as wealth management, currency exchange, and safe deposit boxes. Traditional banking functions include accepting deposits from the public, creating demand deposits, and lending money. Banks are a cornerstone of the economy, facilitating the flow of funds from savers to borrowers, thereby fostering economic growth and development.

Banks operate under a regulatory framework set by national and international authorities to ensure stability, transparency, and trust in the financial system. Their fundamental purpose is to provide a secure environment for individuals and businesses to manage their money while earning a profit through interest on loans and investments.

Definition:

1. "A bank is an institution that makes to grow the money by receiving deposits, making loans, and investing the capital." -John Stuart Mill

Source: Principles of Political Economy (1848)

2. "A bank is a financial institution that accepts deposits from the public and creates credit. Lending activities can be directly performed by the bank or indirectly through capital markets."

Source: Federal Reserve Bank educational materials

"Banks are financial intermediaries that offer the widest range of financial services—especially credit, savings, and payment services—and perform the widest variety of financial functions of any business firm in the economy." -Peter S. Rose Source: Commercial Bank Management (2003)

1.2. History of Indian Banking System

The history of Indian banking is a journey through centuries of transformation, growth, and resilience. From ancient times to the modern era, Indian banks have evolved significantly, shaping the financial landscape of the nation. This narrative captures the key milestones in the history of Indian banking.

A. Ancient and Medieval Periods

The origins of banking in India can be traced back to ancient times, where rudimentary banking activities were conducted by indigenous bankers called "Seths" or "Shroffs." These individuals engaged in money lending and currency exchange. Ancient texts such as the Manusmriti and Arthashastra also mention banking practices, indicating that the concept of banking existed in India over 2000 years ago.

During the medieval period, banking activities were primarily conducted by merchants and moneylenders. The period saw the emergence of indigenous banking houses in different parts of India, like the Chettiars in South India, Marwaris in Western India, and Multanis in North India. These bankers played a crucial role in financing trade and commerce, especially in the absence of formal banking institutions.

B. Colonial Era: The Birth of Modern Banking

The colonial period marked the beginning of formal banking in India with the establishment of the Bank of Hindustan in 1770 in Calcutta (now Kolkata) by Alexander and Co. Although this bank ceased operations in the early 1830s, it set the stage for the development of modern banking in India.

The early 19th century witnessed the establishment of three presidency banks: the Bank of Bengal in 1806, the Bank of Bombay in 1840, and the Bank of Madras in 1843. These banks were established under charters from the British East India Company and served as the principal banking institutions of British India. They primarily catered to the needs of the British administration and European businesses.

In 1921, the three presidency banks were merged to form the Imperial Bank of India, which later became the State Bank of India (SBI) in 1955, following nationalization. The Imperial Bank served as a quasi-central bank, performing limited central banking functions before the establishment of the Reserve Bank of India (RBI).

C. Establishment of the Reserve Bank of India

The Reserve Bank of India, the central bank of the country, was established in 1935 under the Reserve Bank of India Act, 1934. The RBI was initially set up as a private entity but was nationalized in 1949. The establishment of the RBI marked a significant milestone in the history of Indian banking, as it assumed the role of regulating and overseeing the banking sector, managing the country's currency and credit system, and implementing monetary policy.

D. Post-Independence Developments

Post-independence, the Indian banking sector underwent significant changes, driven by the need to support the newly independent nation's economic development. The period saw the nationalization of major banks, aimed at ensuring wider reach and inclusion of rural and semi-urban areas in the formal banking system.

In 1949, the Banking Regulation Act was enacted, giving the RBI broad powers to regulate, supervise, and control banks. This legislation provided a framework for the functioning of banks and addressed issues related to bank management, licensing, and mergers.

The nationalization of banks took place in two phases. The first phase occurred in 1969 when the Government of India nationalized 14 major commercial banks, each with deposits exceeding ₹50 crores. The second phase of nationalization occurred in 1980, bringing six more banks under public ownership. The primary objective of nationalization was to ensure that banks serve the needs of development-oriented policies and extend banking services to remote areas.

E. Liberalization and Modernization

The economic liberalization of the 1990s brought about a paradigm shift in the Indian banking sector. The liberalization policies initiated in 1991 under the guidance of then-Finance Minister Dr. Manmohan Singh and Prime Minister P.V. Narasimha Rao aimed at deregulating the economy and promoting private sector participation in banking.

As part of these reforms, the government allowed the entry of new private sector banks

and foreign banks, fostering competition and innovation in the banking industry. This period saw the emergence of prominent private banks such as ICICI Bank, HDFC Bank, and Axis Bank, which introduced new banking technologies and practices.

Technological advancements played a pivotal role in the modernization of Indian banks. The adoption of information technology led to the introduction of ATMs, online banking, mobile banking, and electronic payment systems. These innovations significantly enhanced customer convenience and operational efficiency.

1.3. Significance of Banks

Banks are fundamental to the economic development and stability of any country. They play multiple roles in both the financial system and the broader economy, influencing individual financial health, business growth, and national economic policies. The significance of banks can be understood through their various functions and impacts.

i. Financial Intermediation

Banks act as intermediaries between savers and borrowers. They collect deposits from individuals and businesses that have excess funds and lend these funds to those who need capital. This process of financial intermediation is crucial because it ensures that money is allocated efficiently within the economy, promoting investment and consumption. By channeling funds from savers to borrowers, banks help in optimizing the use of financial resources, fostering economic growth.

ii. Facilitating Payments and Settlements

Banks provide essential payment services that facilitate day-to-day transactions. They offer various instruments such as cheque, credit and debit cards, and electronic funds transfers, making it easier for individuals and businesses to conduct transactions securely and efficiently. The robust payment and settlement systems managed by banks ensure the smooth functioning of the economy by enabling quick and reliable transfer of funds.

iii. Credit Provision and Economic Growth

Access to credit is critical for economic development. Banks provide loans and credit facilities to individuals, businesses, and governments, supporting a wide range of activities from personal consumption to business expansion and infrastructure development. By offering credit, banks enable entrepreneurship and innovation, helping businesses to grow and create jobs. This, in turn, drives economic growth and improves living standards.

iv. Risk Management and Insurance

Banks offer various financial products that help individuals and businesses manage risks. Savings accounts, fixed deposits, and various insurance products provide a safety net against financial uncertainties. By offering risk management tools, banks help protect wealth and ensure financial stability for their customers. Additionally, banks themselves manage risks through diversification and adherence to regulatory requirements, contributing to the overall stability of the financial system.

v. Mobilizing Savings

Banks encourage savings by providing safe and attractive deposit options. They offer interest on deposits, motivating individuals to save rather than spend. This mobilization of savings is vital for economic stability and growth as it provides a pool of funds that can be used for productive investments. By pooling individual savings, banks can lend larger sums to businesses and projects, thus playing a crucial role in capital formation.

vi. Supporting Monetary Policy

Central banks, like the Reserve Bank of India, use commercial banks as conduits for implementing monetary policy. Through mechanisms such as reserve requirements and open market operations, central banks influence the amount of money and credit in the economy. Commercial banks play a pivotal role in this process by adjusting their lending and deposit activities in response to policy changes. This interaction helps maintain economic stability by controlling inflation and fostering growth.

vii. Economic Stabilization

Banks contribute to economic stabilization by managing the flow of funds within the economy. During periods of economic distress, such as recessions, banks can help stabilize the economy by continuing to provide credit and supporting economic activities. Conversely, during periods of high economic growth, banks can help prevent overheating by tightening credit conditions. By responding to economic cycles, banks play a critical role in smoothing out economic fluctuations and maintaining stability.

viii. Promoting Financial Inclusion

Banks are instrumental in promoting financial inclusion, ensuring that a wide range of financial services is accessible to all segments of the population, including the underserved and unbanked. Initiatives such as opening basic savings accounts, offering microfinance, and providing financial literacy programs help integrate more people into the formal financial system. Financial inclusion not only improves individual livelihoods but also contributes to broader economic development by increasing overall savings and investment rates.

ix. Enhancing International Trade and Investment

Banks facilitate international trade and investment by providing services such as foreign exchange, letters of credit, and trade finance. These services help businesses manage the complexities and risks associated with international transactions. By supporting cross-border trade and investment, banks contribute to global economic integration and growth. They enable businesses to expand their markets and access new opportunities, driving economic development.

x. Building Infrastructure and Development

Banks play a crucial role in financing infrastructure projects such as roads, bridges, and power plants. These projects require substantial investment, which is often provided through long-term loans and bonds issued by banks. By funding infrastructure development, banks contribute to improving the quality of life, enhancing productivity, and supporting sustainable economic growth.

1.4 Types of Banks

Banks play a crucial role in the financial system by providing a wide range of services to individuals, businesses, and governments. Different types of banks serve various purposes, and understanding these differences can help individuals and businesses make informed financial decisions. We explore several types of banks, each with its unique functions and characteristics.

1. **Commercial Banks**
2. **Cooperative Banks**
3. **Regional Rural Banks (RRBs)**
4. **Agricultural and Rural Development Banks**
5. **Development Banks**
6. **Central Banks**

1.4.1 Commercial Banks

Commercial banks are the backbone of the modern financial system, offering a wide array of services to individuals, businesses, and governments. They serve as the primary conduit for channeling funds from savers to borrowers, thereby facilitating economic activity and growth. Commercial banks are the most common type of banks and form the backbone of the banking system. They provide a wide range of financial services to individuals, businesses, and governments. There are two main categories of commercial banks in India:

Functions of Commercial Banks

Commercial banks are central to the financial system and perform a variety of functions that are crucial for economic activity. These functions range from traditional banking services to modern financial solutions. Let's delve into the primary functions of commercial banks:

i. Accepting Deposits

Commercial banks serve as custodians of funds by accepting deposits from individuals, businesses, and other entities. These deposits may include:

- **Savings Accounts**: Deposits meant for saving money, typically earning interest.
- **Current Accounts**: Deposits that facilitate frequent transactions without restrictions on withdrawals.
- **Fixed Deposits**: Deposits with a fixed tenure and predetermined interest rates, offering higher returns.

By accepting deposits, commercial banks provide a safe and secure avenue for individuals to store their money while earning interest on their balances.

ii. Extending Credit

One of the primary functions of commercial banks is to provide credit to borrowers in the form of loans and advances. These loans cater to various needs, including:

- **Personal Loans**: Funds provided for personal expenses such as education, medical emergencies, or weddings.
- **Business Loans**: Capital provided to businesses for expansion, working capital, or investment in assets.
- **Home Loans**: Financing for purchasing or constructing residential properties.
- **Vehicle Loans**: Funding for purchasing automobiles or other vehicles.

Commercial banks assess the creditworthiness of borrowers based on factors such as income, credit history, and collateral before extending credit facilities.

iii. Facilitating Payments

Commercial banks facilitate the transfer of funds between individuals, businesses, and institutions through various payment services. These include:

- **Cheque Clearing**: Processing and clearing of cheque issued by customers for payments.
- **Electronic Fund Transfers (EFTs)**: Transfer of funds electronically between accounts, including NEFT, RTGS, and IMPS.
- **Debit and Credit Cards**: Providing cards for making purchases and withdrawals, both online and offline.
- **Mobile and Internet Banking**: Offering digital platforms for conducting banking transactions remotely.

By providing efficient payment services, commercial banks enable seamless financial transactions, enhancing convenience and accessibility for customers.

iv. Investment Banking Services

Commercial banks engage in investment banking activities to facilitate capital market transactions and corporate finance. These services include:

- **Underwriting**: Assisting companies in raising capital by underwriting securities issuance, such as initial public offerings (IPOs) or bond offerings.
- **Merger and Acquisition (M&A) Advisory**: Providing advice and assistance to companies involved in mergers, acquisitions, and corporate restructuring.
- **Corporate Finance**: Offering financial advisory services for capital structuring, project financing, and strategic investments.

Through their investment banking divisions, commercial banks help businesses access capital markets and navigate complex financial transactions.

v. Wealth Management

Commercial banks offer wealth management services to high-net-worth individuals and institutional clients. These services include:

- **Portfolio Management**: Designing and managing investment portfolios tailored to individual risk preferences and financial goals.
- **Financial Planning**: Providing comprehensive financial planning services covering areas such as retirement planning, tax optimization, and estate planning.
- **Private Banking**: Offering specialized banking services, investment advice, and personalized financial solutions to affluent clients.

By offering wealth management services, commercial banks help clients grow and preserve their wealth over the long term.

vi. Foreign Exchange Services

Commercial banks facilitate foreign exchange transactions to meet the currency needs of customers engaged in international trade and travel. These services include:

- **Currency Exchange**: Buying and selling foreign currencies to facilitate international transactions.
- **Trade Finance**: Providing financing and risk mitigation solutions for importers and exporters, such as letters of credit and trade finance facilities.
- **Remittances**: Facilitating cross-border fund transfers for individuals sending money to family members or making international payments.

Through their foreign exchange desks, commercial banks support global trade and enable seamless cross-border transactions.

1.4.2 Cooperative Banks

Cooperative banks, rooted in the principles of cooperation and mutual assistance, serve as pillars of community-centric finance. Embracing inclusivity and democratic ownership, they offer tailored financial services to empower members and foster local economic development. These banks prioritize the needs of their communities, providing accessible savings, credit, and banking solutions to promote financial inclusion and social cohesion. With a focus on cooperative values and member participation, cooperative banks play a pivotal role in building resilient and sustainable economies.

A. Functions of Cooperative Banks

Cooperative banks are unique financial institutions that operate on the principles of cooperation, self-help, and mutual assistance. They cater to the specific needs of their members and communities, focusing on providing affordable financial services and promoting financial inclusion. Here are the primary functions of cooperative banks:

i. Mobilizing Savings:

Cooperative banks encourage members of their community to save money by offering various deposit products. These deposits typically come with attractive interest rates and flexible terms, making them accessible to individuals from all walks of life. By mobilizing savings from their members, cooperative banks create a pool of funds that can be used for lending and investment within the community.

ii. Providing Credit Facilities:

One of the key functions of cooperative banks is to provide credit facilities to their members for a variety of purposes. These may include:

- **Personal Loans**: Funds provided to members for personal expenses such as education, healthcare, or emergencies.
- **Agricultural Loans**: Credit extended to farmers for crop cultivation, farm equipment purchases, or agricultural infrastructure development.
- **Small Business Loans**: Financing for micro, small, and medium enterprises (MSMEs) to support entrepreneurship and local economic development.
- **Housing Loans**: Assistance provided to members for purchasing or constructing homes or improving housing conditions.

Cooperative banks tailor their loan products to meet the specific needs of their members, offering competitive interest rates and flexible repayment terms.

iii. Promoting Financial Inclusion:

Cooperative banks play a crucial role in promoting financial inclusion by extending banking services to underserved and marginalized segments of society. They often operate in rural and semi-urban areas where traditional banks may be less accessible. By offering basic banking services such as savings accounts, loans, and payment facilities, cooperative banks help empower individuals and communities economically.

iv. Supporting Agricultural and Rural Development:

Many cooperative banks have a strong focus on agriculture and rural development, reflecting the needs of their local communities. They provide financial support to farmers, agricultural cooperatives, and rural enterprises, contributing to agricultural productivity, income generation, and livelihood enhancement. Cooperative banks may offer specialized products and services tailored to the unique requirements of the agricultural sector, such as crop loans, livestock loans, and farm machinery financing.

v. Facilitating Community Development:

Cooperative banks often serve as catalysts for community development initiatives, leveraging their resources and networks to address social and economic challenges. They may collaborate with local authorities, non-profit organizations, and community groups to implement projects and programs aimed at improving education, healthcare, sanitation, and infrastructure in their operating areas. By actively engaging in community development efforts, cooperative banks strengthen their ties with members and contribute to the overall well-being of society.

vi. **Participating in Cooperative Movement:**

Cooperative banks are integral components of the broader cooperative movement, which emphasizes democratic control, member participation, and community ownership. They actively promote the principles of cooperation and mutual assistance among their members, fostering a sense of solidarity and collective responsibility. Cooperative banks may collaborate with other cooperative enterprises, including agricultural cooperatives, consumer cooperatives, and housing cooperatives, to advance shared goals and values.

B. Types of Cooperative Banks

In India, cooperative banks are an integral part of the financial system, catering to the needs of various sections of society, particularly in rural and semi-urban areas. They are governed by both state and central cooperative laws and regulations. The structure of cooperative banks in India can be broadly categorized into two types: Urban Cooperative Banks (UCBs) and Rural Cooperative Credit Institutions.

1. Urban Cooperative Banks (UCBs)

Urban Cooperative Banks (UCBs) operate in urban and semi-urban areas and cater to the banking needs of small businesses, industries, and urban households. They can be further divided into:

- **Scheduled UCBs**: These are included in the Second Schedule of the Reserve Bank of India (RBI) Act, 1934, and are eligible for certain privileges, including access to inter-bank borrowings and borrowing from the RBI.
- **Non-Scheduled UCBs**: These do not enjoy the same privileges as scheduled banks and generally operate on a smaller scale.

2. Rural Cooperative Credit Institutions

Rural Cooperative Credit Institutions primarily serve the rural population, including farmers and small-scale rural enterprises. They are structured in a three-tier system:

I. Short-Term Cooperative Credit Institutions

a. Primary Agricultural Credit Societies (PACS):

- These are the grassroots-level cooperative credit institutions.
- They cater to the short-term and medium-term credit needs of the rural population.
- PACS are affiliated with District Central Cooperative Banks (DCCBs).

b. District Central Cooperative Banks (DCCBs):

- These operate at the district level.
- They provide credit to PACS and serve individual borrowers.
- DCCBs are further affiliated with State Cooperative Banks (StCBs).

c. State Cooperative Banks (StCBs):

- These operate at the state level.
- They act as a federation for DCCBs in the state.
- StCBs provide a link between the cooperative credit structure and the RBI.

II. Long-Term Cooperative Credit Institutions

a. State Cooperative Agriculture and Rural Development Banks (SCARDBs):

- These provide long-term credit for agricultural development, infrastructure, and rural development projects.
- SCARDBs operate at the state level and are federations of Primary Cooperative Agriculture and Rural Development Banks (PCARDBs).

b. Primary Cooperative Agriculture and Rural Development Banks (PCARDBs):

- These operate at the primary level and provide long-term loans to farmers and rural enterprises for developmental purposes.

1.4.3 Regional Rural Banks (RRBs)

Regional Rural Banks (RRBs) are a unique form of financial institution in India, established to provide credit and other financial services to the rural population, particularly to small and marginal farmers, agricultural laborers, artisans, and small entrepreneurs. RRBs were created under the Regional Rural Banks Act, 1976, with the aim of developing the rural economy by ensuring the provision of institutional credit.

Functions of Regional Rural Banks (RRBs)

i. Provision of Agricultural Credit: One of the primary functions of RRBs is to provide credit facilities to the agricultural sector. This includes short-term, medium-term, and long-term loans to farmers for various agricultural activities, such as purchasing seeds, fertilizers, and agricultural machinery, as well as for irrigation and other farm development projects.

ii. Promotion of Rural Development: RRBs play a significant role in promoting rural development. They provide financial support for various rural development activities, including the establishment of small-scale industries, cottage industries, and rural crafts. This helps in generating employment and improving the standard of living in rural areas.

iii. Support for Small and Marginal Farmers: RRBs focus on providing financial assistance to small and marginal farmers who often have limited access to traditional banking services. By offering tailored financial products and services, RRBs help these farmers improve their agricultural productivity and income.

iv. Microfinance and Self-Help Groups (SHGs): RRBs actively participate in microfinance initiatives and support Self-Help Groups (SHGs). They provide small loans to SHGs, which are often formed by rural women, to undertake various income-generating activities. This promotes financial inclusion and empowerment of rural women.

v. Deposit Mobilization: RRBs accept deposits from the rural population, encouraging savings among rural households. They offer various deposit schemes, such as savings accounts, fixed deposits, and recurring deposits, which help inculcate a savings habit among the rural populace.

vi. Financial Inclusion: RRBs are instrumental in promoting financial inclusion by extending banking services to unbanked and underbanked rural areas. They set up branches in remote regions, providing access to basic banking services such as savings, credit, remittance, and insurance.

vii. Implementation of Government Schemes: RRBs are key partners in the implementation of various government schemes aimed at rural development and poverty alleviation. They play a crucial role in the disbursement of subsidies, grants, and other financial aids under schemes such as the Pradhan Mantri Awas Yojana (PMAY), Pradhan Mantri Fasal Bima Yojana (PMFBY), and the Mahatma Gandhi National Rural Employment Guarantee Act (MGNREGA).

viii. Development of Rural Infrastructure: RRBs contribute to the development of rural infrastructure by financing projects related to rural roads, bridges, schools, and healthcare facilities. This aids in the overall socio-economic development of rural areas.

ix. Providing Non-Farm Credit: Apart from agricultural credit, RRBs also provide loans for non-farm activities, including retail trade, transport, and small businesses. This diversification helps in reducing the dependence of the rural population on agriculture alone and encourages them to explore other income-generating activities.

1.4.4 Agricultural and Rural Development Banks

Agricultural and Rural Development Banks (ARDBs) in India play a crucial role in supporting the agricultural sector and promoting rural development. These banks focus on providing long-term credit for agricultural and rural infrastructure projects. They include State Cooperative Agriculture and Rural Development Banks (SCARDBs) and Primary Cooperative Agriculture and Rural Development Banks (PCARDBs).

Functions of Agricultural and Rural Development Banks (ARDBs)

i. Provision of Long-Term Credit for Agriculture: ARDBs provide long-term loans to farmers for various agricultural purposes. These loans are essential for the purchase of agricultural machinery, equipment, and inputs, as well as for land development, irrigation projects, and the construction of storage facilities. Long-term credit helps farmers make substantial investments in their farms, leading to increased productivity and income.

ii. Financing Rural Infrastructure Projects: One of the primary functions of ARDBs is to finance the development of rural infrastructure. This includes the construction and maintenance of rural roads, bridges, irrigation systems, and drainage facilities. By improving rural infrastructure, ARDBs facilitate better connectivity, access to markets, and overall economic development in rural areas.

iii. Support for Allied Agricultural Activities: ARDBs provide financial assistance for allied agricultural activities such as dairy farming, poultry farming, fisheries, and horticulture. These activities are crucial for diversifying farmers' income sources and ensuring food security. Loans for these purposes help farmers invest in livestock, feed, and other necessary resources.

iv. Promoting Rural Industries: ARDBs play a significant role in promoting rural industries and small-scale enterprises. They offer credit facilities to artisans, craftsmen, and small entrepreneurs for establishing and expanding rural industries. This support helps in generating employment opportunities and promoting economic activities beyond traditional farming.

v. Development of Agro-Based Industries: ARDBs provide financial support for the establishment and modernization of agro-based industries such as food processing units, cold storage facilities, and agro-processing plants. These industries add value to agricultural produce, reduce post-harvest losses, and create additional income streams for farmers.

vi. Encouraging Sustainable Agricultural Practices: ARDBs promote sustainable agricultural practices by providing loans for organic farming, integrated pest management, and the adoption of environmentally friendly technologies. By encouraging sustainable practices, ARDBs help farmers reduce their environmental impact and improve the long-term viability of agriculture.

vii. Financial Inclusion and Empowerment: ARDBs play a crucial role in enhancing financial inclusion in rural areas. They provide banking services to unbanked and underbanked populations, offering savings accounts, fixed deposits, and other financial products. By bringing more people into the formal banking system, ARDBs empower rural communities and promote economic stability.

viii. Implementation of Government Schemes: ARDBs are key partners in implementing various government schemes aimed at rural development and agricultural enhancement. They help disburse funds and subsidies under programs like the Pradhan Mantri Krishi Sinchai Yojana (PMKSY) and the National Rural Employment Guarantee Act (NREGA), ensuring that the benefits reach the intended beneficiaries.

ix. Technical and Advisory Services: Beyond financial assistance, ARDBs provide technical and advisory services to farmers and rural entrepreneurs. They offer guidance on best agricultural practices, new technologies, and business management, helping clients make informed decisions and improve their productivity and profitability.

x. Capacity Building and Skill Development: ARDBs invest in capacity building and skill development programs for farmers and rural youth. They conduct training sessions, workshops, and seminars to enhance the skills and knowledge of rural populations, enabling them to adopt modern agricultural techniques and entrepreneurial ventures.

1.4.5 Development Banks

Development Banks are financial institutions established with the primary aim of providing long-term capital for economic development projects. They play a crucial role in fostering industrial growth, infrastructure development, and the overall economic advancement of a country. These banks are essential in bridging the gap between the demand for and supply of capital for developmental purposes, particularly in sectors where private commercial banks might be reluctant to invest due to higher risks and lower immediate returns.

Functions of Development Banks

i. Provision of Long-Term Finance: Development banks provide long-term financing for large-scale projects, including infrastructure development, industrial projects, and other capital-intensive ventures. These loans often have longer maturity periods compared to those offered by commercial banks, enabling businesses to undertake substantial investments without the pressure of short-term repayment.

ii. Promotion of Industrial Growth: One of the primary functions of development banks is to promote industrial development. They provide financial assistance to new and existing industries for expansion, modernization, and technological upgrades. This support helps in boosting industrial output and competitiveness, contributing to the overall economic growth.

iii. Infrastructure Development: Development banks play a pivotal role in financing infrastructure projects such as roads, bridges, ports, power plants, and telecommunications. By providing the necessary capital for these projects, they help in building the backbone of the economy, facilitating trade, and improving the quality of life for citizens.

iv. Support for Small and Medium Enterprises (SMEs): Recognizing the vital role of SMEs in economic development and employment generation, development banks offer targeted financial products and services to support these enterprises. This includes providing credit, guarantees, and advisory services tailored to the needs of SMEs, thereby helping them grow and thrive.

v. Promotion of Regional Development: Development banks often focus on reducing regional disparities by financing projects in less developed areas. By channeling investments into underdeveloped regions, they stimulate economic activities, create jobs, and promote balanced regional growth.

vi. Encouraging Innovation and Technology Development: Development banks support research and development (R&D) activities and the adoption of new technologies. They provide funding for innovative projects and startups that have the potential to drive economic transformation and foster a knowledge-based economy.

vii. Project Appraisal and Advisory Services: Besides providing finance, development banks offer project appraisal and advisory services. They evaluate the technical, economic, and financial viability of proposed projects, ensuring that funded projects are sustainable and have a high probability of success. This advisory role helps in mitigating risks and improving project outcomes.

viii. Support for Sustainable Development: Development banks increasingly focus on financing projects that promote sustainable development. This includes investments in renewable energy, energy efficiency, environmental conservation, and sustainable agriculture. By supporting green projects, development banks contribute to the fight against climate change and environmental degradation.

ix. Facilitating Foreign Investment: Development banks often play a crucial role in attracting foreign investment by providing guarantees, joint financing, and creating a favorable investment climate. They collaborate with international financial institutions, fostering cross-border investments and economic cooperation.

x. Capital Market Development: Development banks contribute to the development of capital markets by underwriting and subscribing to securities, providing venture capital, and supporting the issuance of bonds. Their involvement in capital markets helps in mobilizing resources for development projects and enhancing financial market stability.

Major Development Banks of India

India has several major development banks that play a crucial role in financing and fostering economic development. These institutions provide long-term capital for industrial growth, infrastructure projects, and various other developmental activities. Here are some of the major development banks in India:

1. Industrial Development Bank of India (IDBI)

The Industrial Development Bank of India (IDBI) was established in 1964 as a subsidiary of the Reserve Bank of India (RBI). It was later transformed into a full-fledged development bank. IDBI provides financial assistance for industrial growth through a variety of financial products, including term loans, working capital loans, and project finance. In 2004, IDBI was converted into a commercial bank, but it continues to play a significant role in industrial financing.

2. National Bank for Agriculture and Rural Development (NABARD)

The National Bank for Agriculture and Rural Development (NABARD) is a crucial institution in India's rural development landscape. Established on July 12, 1982, under the National Bank for Agriculture and Rural Development Act 1981, NABARD's primary mandate is to promote sustainable and equitable agriculture and rural development through effective credit support, related services, institution building, and other innovative initiatives.

Functions of NABARD

i. Credit Provision and Refinancing: NABARD plays a pivotal role in providing credit to the agricultural and rural sectors. It refinances financial institutions that provide loans to agriculture, small-scale industries, cottage and village industries, handicrafts, and other rural crafts. This helps in ensuring a steady flow of credit to these crucial sectors, promoting their growth and sustainability.

ii. Developmental and Promotional Activities: NABARD undertakes various developmental and promotional initiatives aimed at fostering rural development. This includes funding for infrastructure projects like roads, bridges, irrigation, and storage facilities. NABARD also supports projects that promote innovative agricultural practices, sustainable farming, and capacity building of rural communities.

iii. Supervision and Regulation: NABARD supervises and regulates cooperative banks and regional rural banks (RRBs) to ensure they operate efficiently and adhere to financial norms and standards. This supervisory role helps maintain the financial health and stability of these institutions, which are critical for rural credit delivery.

iv. Financial Inclusion and Microfinance: NABARD is actively involved in promoting financial inclusion in rural areas. It supports the establishment and operation of self-help groups (SHGs), joint liability groups (JLGs), and other community-based organizations that provide microfinance services. These initiatives help in extending banking services to the unbanked population and promote economic activities at the grassroots level.

v. Rural Infrastructure Development: Through the Rural Infrastructure Development Fund (RIDF), NABARD provides loans to state governments and state-owned corporations for the development of rural infrastructure. This includes projects related to irrigation, rural roads, rural bridges, health, and education infrastructure. The RIDF is instrumental in enhancing the quality of life and economic opportunities in rural areas.

vi. Climate and Sustainable Development: NABARD is involved in initiatives aimed at climate adaptation and sustainable development. It manages funds such as the National Adaptation Fund for Climate Change (NAFCC) and the Green Climate Fund (GCF), which finance projects to combat climate change and promote sustainable agricultural practices.

vii. Research and Development: NABARD conducts and supports research in agriculture and rural development. It funds studies, surveys, and pilot projects that provide insights into rural economies and inform policy-making. This research function helps in identifying challenges and opportunities in the rural sector and devising effective strategies to address them.

3. Small Industries Development Bank of India (SIDBI)

SIDBI was established in 1990 to provide financial assistance to micro, small, and medium enterprises (MSMEs). It offers a wide range of financial services, including direct loans, refinancing, and equity support. SIDBI plays a crucial role in promoting the growth and development of the MSME sector in India, which is a key driver of employment and economic activity.

4. Export-Import Bank of India (Exim Bank)

The Export-Import Bank of India (Exim Bank) was established in 1982 to finance, facilitate, and promote foreign trade. Exim Bank provides financial assistance for Indian exporters and importers, as well as for overseas investment by Indian companies. It offers a range of services, including export credit, project finance, and guarantees, to support India's international trade.

5. National Housing Bank (NHB)

Established in 1988, the National Housing Bank (NHB) is a wholly-owned subsidiary of the Reserve Bank of India. NHB's primary objective is to promote housing finance institutions and enhance the credit flow for housing. It provides financial support to various housing finance companies, cooperatives, and banks, thereby fostering affordable housing development across the country.

6. Infrastructure Development Finance Company (IDFC)

IDFC was established in 1997 to provide finance for infrastructure projects. It supports the development of various infrastructure sectors, including transportation, energy, water, and telecommunications. IDFC offers project finance, advisory services, and investment banking to facilitate the development of sustainable infrastructure.

7. India Infrastructure Finance Company Limited (IIFCL)

IIFCL was established in 2006 to provide long-term financial assistance for infrastructure projects in India. It aims to promote public-private partnerships (PPPs) in infrastructure development by offering financial products such as loans, refinancing, and take-out financing. IIFCL supports projects in sectors like transportation, energy, water, and urban infrastructure.

8. Industrial Finance Corporation of India (IFCI)

IFCI is one of the oldest development banks in India, established in 1948. It provides financial support for industrial development through term loans, working capital loans, and project finance. IFCI has been instrumental in financing various large-scale industrial projects and promoting industrial growth in the country.

Key aspects take away from Unit 1

Definition of Banks:

- Banks are financial institutions that accept deposits from the public and provide loans and other financial services.
- They play a crucial role in the economy by facilitating the flow of funds between savers and borrowers, promoting investment, and supporting economic growth.

History of Indian Banks:

- The history of banking in India dates back to ancient times, with evidence of banking practices found in texts like the Arthashastra.
- Modern banking in India began with the establishment of the Bank of Hindustan in 1770 and the General Bank of India in 1786.
- The Reserve Bank of India (RBI) was established in 1935 as the central banking authority, regulating and supervising banks in India.

Significance of Banks:

- Banks play a crucial role in the economy by mobilizing savings and channeling them into productive investments.
- They provide a range of financial services, including credit, deposits, payment services, and risk management, which are essential for economic activities.
- Banks contribute to economic growth by providing capital to businesses, promoting entrepreneurship, and facilitating trade and commerce.

Types of Banks:

Commercial Banks:

- Commercial banks are the most common type of banks that provide a wide range of financial services to individuals, businesses, and governments.
- They include public sector banks, private sector banks, and foreign banks operating in India.

Cooperative Banks:

- Cooperative banks are owned and operated by their members, who are typically individuals or organizations within a specific community or profession.
- They focus on providing financial services to their members and promoting the economic interests of the community.

Regional Rural Banks (RRBs):

- RRBs were established to provide credit and other financial services to rural areas, particularly to small farmers, artisans, and rural entrepreneurs.
- They operate in collaboration with the central government, state governments, and sponsor banks.

Agricultural and Rural Development Banks:

- These banks specialize in providing financial assistance for agriculture and rural development projects.
- They include institutions like NABARD, which support agricultural credit, rural infrastructure development, and other rural initiatives.

Development Banks:

- Development banks are specialized financial institutions that focus on providing long-term capital for economic development projects.
- They support sectors such as industry, infrastructure, exports, and small businesses, contributing to overall economic growth and development.

Check Your Progress

Exercise

A. Answer the following in brief. (Short Notes)

1. What distinguishes Regional Rural Banks (RRBs) from other types of banks?
2. Name one specialized bank that focuses on providing financial assistance for agriculture and rural development projects.
3. What is the primary function of development banks?
4. Why are banks considered crucial for economic growth?
5. What role do banks play in mobilizing savings?
6. How do banks facilitate the flow of funds in an economy?
7. What are the key services provided by banks to their customers?
8. When did modern banking in India begin?
9. Name one of the earliest banks established in India during the colonial period.
10. What are the main types of commercial banks operating in India?
11. Describe the primary function of cooperative banks.
12. What distinguishes Regional Rural Banks (RRBs) from other types of banks?

A. Answer the following in detail. (Long answer type question)

1. Compare and contrast the functions and characteristics of commercial banks, cooperative banks, and specialized banks in India. Provide examples to illustrate the differences.
2. Discuss the unique features and objectives of Regional Rural Banks (RRBs) and Agricultural and Rural Development Banks in India. How do these institutions contribute to rural

development and agricultural finance?

3. Analyze the role of development banks in financing long-term development projects and promoting economic growth in India. What are the major challenges faced by development banks in fulfilling their mandate?
4. Discuss the importance of banks in mobilizing savings and channeling them into productive investments. How does this process contribute to capital formation and economic growth?
5. Explain how banks facilitate entrepreneurship and support the growth of small and medium-sized enterprises (SMEs) through access to credit and other financial services.
6. Evaluate the role of banks in promoting financial inclusion and reducing poverty by providing banking services to underserved and marginalized sections of society.
7. Trace the evolution of banking in India from ancient times to the modern era, highlighting significant milestones and developments.
8. Analyze the impact of colonial rule on the banking system in India. Discuss the establishment of the Reserve Bank of India (RBI) and its role in shaping the Indian banking sector.
9. Discuss the various financial services offered by banks and their significance in meeting the diverse needs of individuals, businesses, and governments.
10. How do banks serve as intermediaries between savers and borrowers? Describe the process of deposit mobilization and credit creation by banks in detail.

Chapter 02

Central Bank and Universal Banking System

2.1. Meaning of Central Bank

Central banks typically operate independently of the government and are tasked with ensuring the stability and efficiency of the financial system. They are responsible for formulating and implementing monetary policy, which involves setting interest rates, regulating the money supply, and managing exchange rates. Central banks also oversee the banking sector, monitor financial markets, and often act as the government's banker and financial advisor.

Definitions of Central Banks

Milton Friedman: "A central bank is an institution that controls the money supply and interest rates in a country, often with broad authority to implement monetary policy in order to achieve macroeconomic goals such as price stability and full employment."

Ben Bernanke: "Central banks are financial institutions with the primary responsibility of managing the nation's money supply and credit conditions. They aim to promote economic stability and growth by controlling inflation, stabilizing currency values, and ensuring the smooth functioning of the financial system."

Alan Greenspan: "Central banks are the guardians of the nation's monetary system, responsible for overseeing the banking system, regulating financial institutions, and maintaining the stability of the currency. They wield significant influence over the economy through their control of interest rates and monetary policy tools."

Paul Volcker: "Central banks are the cornerstone of a country's monetary and financial system, entrusted with the responsibility of maintaining price stability, fostering economic growth, and safeguarding the integrity of the financial markets. They serve as the lender of last resort and play a critical role in times of crisis."

John Maynard Keynes: "A central bank is the pivot around which the modern capitalist economy revolves. It is the institution responsible for managing the nation's money supply, controlling interest rates, and regulating the banking system. Central banks play a crucial role in stabilizing the economy and preventing financial crises."

2.2. History of Reserve Bank of India

The Reserve Bank of India (RBI), established in 1935, stands as the cornerstone of India's monetary and financial system, reflecting a rich history deeply intertwined with the nation's economic journey. Born out of the imperative need for a central banking authority during the pre-independence era, the RBI's inception marked a pivotal moment in India's quest for financial stability and economic development. From its modest beginnings in Kolkata (then Calcutta) under the stewardship of Sir Osborne Smith, the RBI swiftly emerged as a vital institution tasked with regulating the issuance of currency, managing the monetary framework, and steering the nascent economy towards prosperity. Post-independence, the RBI's role expanded exponentially, relocating its headquarters to Mumbai (then Bombay) and assuming a broader mandate encompassing the supervision of the banking sector and the promotion of economic growth. Over the decades, the RBI has navigated through significant milestones, adapting to shifting economic paradigms and global challenges while remaining steadfast in its commitment to safeguarding monetary stability and fostering inclusive growth. Today, as India strides towards a digital future and grapples with the complexities of a dynamic global economy, the RBI continues to serve as a beacon of stability and resilience, shaping the trajectory of India's economic landscape with foresight and diligence.

A. Pre-Independence Era:

The pre-independence era marked the genesis of the Reserve Bank of India (RBI) amidst discussions and proposals for the establishment of a central bank in India. In the early 20th century, the need for a formal banking institution to regulate the monetary system became apparent. Various committees and commissions, including the Royal Commission on Indian Currency and Finance (1926), advocated for the creation of a central bank. These deliberations culminated in the enactment of the Reserve Bank of India Act in 1934 by the British Parliament, which provided the legal framework for the establishment and functioning of the RBI. Officially inaugurated on April 1, 1935, with Sir Osborne Smith as its first Governor, the RBI was tasked with regulating the issuance of banknotes, managing the currency system, and controlling monetary policy in India.

B. Post-Independence Era:

Following India's independence in 1947, the Reserve Bank of India entered a new phase characterized by the relocation of its headquarters from Kolkata to Mumbai (then Bombay). This period witnessed the expansion of the RBI's functions beyond its initial responsibilities. It played a pivotal role in regulating and supervising the banking sector, developing money and capital markets, and promoting economic growth in the newly independent nation. The nationalization of 14 major banks in 1969 brought them under the control of the RBI, amplifying its influence in shaping India's banking landscape. Throughout the 1950s and 1960s, the RBI mobilized resources for priority sectors, facilitated financial inclusion, and supported the country's economic development initiatives.

C. Economic Reforms and Liberalization:

The 1980s and 1990s ushered in a new era of economic reforms and liberalization in India, signaling significant changes in the role and functions of the Reserve Bank of India. As the country embraced globalization and sought to integrate its economy with the global market, the RBI adapted its monetary policy framework to stabilize the economy, manage inflation, and promote financial sector reforms. The adoption of market-oriented policies aimed to enhance efficiency, competitiveness, and transparency in the financial system. During this period, the RBI played a critical role in steering the economy through various challenges, including external shocks and internal reforms, while maintaining its focus on monetary stability and financial sector development.

D. Modernization and Technological Advancements:

In the 21st century, the Reserve Bank of India embarked on a journey of modernization and technological advancements to meet the evolving needs of India's rapidly growing economy and increasingly complex financial landscape. Embracing digitalization and innovation, the RBI focused on upgrading the banking infrastructure, enhancing regulatory frameworks, and adopting cutting-edge technologies to improve efficiency, transparency, and resilience in the financial system. As the central institution in India's economic and financial ecosystem, the RBI continued to play a proactive role in managing economic challenges, including the global financial crisis of 2008 and the COVID-19 pandemic, while pursuing its mandate of ensuring monetary stability, financial inclusion, and sustainable economic growth.

2.3. Functions of Reserve Bank of India

Reserve banks, often referred to as central banks, play a pivotal role in a country's monetary system. While the specific functions may vary slightly depending on the country, here are the primary functions typically associated with reserve banks:

i. Monetary Policy Formulation and Implementation: One of the primary functions of a reserve bank is to formulate and execute monetary policy. This involves managing key interest rates, such as the central bank's lending rate (like the Federal Funds Rate in the US) and reserve requirements, to influence money supply, inflation, and economic growth.

ii. Issuance of Currency: Reserve banks are usually responsible for issuing and managing a country's currency. They ensure an adequate supply of physical currency notes and coins in circulation, as well as maintaining the security and integrity of the currency.

iii. Banker to the Government: Reserve banks often act as bankers to the government, providing various banking services such as managing government accounts, facilitating transactions, and underwriting government debt issuance.

iv. Banker to Commercial Banks: Reserve banks serve as bankers to commercial banks within the country. They maintain accounts for commercial banks, facilitate interbank transactions, provide liquidity support, and supervise and regulate the banking system.

v. Lender of Last Resort: In times of financial crisis or liquidity shortages, reserve banks act as lenders of last resort. They provide emergency liquidity assistance to financial institutions to prevent systemic disruptions and maintain stability in the financial system.

vi. Regulation and Supervision: Reserve banks often have regulatory and supervisory authority over financial institutions operating within their jurisdiction. They establish and enforce regulations to ensure the safety, soundness, and stability of the banking and financial system.

vii. Foreign Exchange Management: Reserve banks manage the country's foreign exchange reserves and formulate policies to stabilize the exchange rate. They may intervene in the foreign exchange market to influence the value of the domestic currency or to address imbalances in the balance of payments.

viii. Collection and Analysis of Economic Data: Reserve banks collect, analyze, and publish a wide range of economic data relevant to monetary policy formulation and decision-making. This includes data on inflation, employment, GDP growth, and financial market developments.

ix. Financial Stability Oversight: Reserve banks monitor and assess risks to financial stability, including systemic risks arising from the activities of financial institutions, markets, and infrastructures. They may take measures to address emerging threats to financial stability and promote resilience in the financial system.

x. Payment System Oversight: Reserve banks oversee payment and settlement systems to ensure their efficiency, safety, and reliability. They establish and enforce rules and standards for payment systems, promote the adoption of innovative payment technologies, and mitigate risks associated with payment and settlement activities.

2.4 Universal Banking System, ADRs and GDRs

A universal banking system refers to a banking model where a single financial institution offers a comprehensive range of banking and financial services, including commercial banking, investment banking, and asset management, under one roof.

Universal banking systems offer various advantages and disadvantages, reflecting the complexities and trade-offs inherent in this banking model.

A. Advantages:

i. Diversification of Services: Universal banks can offer a wide range of financial products and services, including commercial banking, investment banking, asset management, and insurance. This diversification allows them to cater to diverse customer needs and generate revenue from multiple sources.

ii. One-Stop Shop: Customers benefit from the convenience of accessing a comprehensive suite of banking and financial services from a single institution. This reduces the need to maintain relationships with multiple financial providers and simplifies financial management.

iii. Cross-Selling Opportunities: Universal banks can leverage their broad range of services to cross-sell products to their existing customer base. For example, a bank's retail banking customers may be offered investment products or insurance policies, leading to increased revenue and customer loyalty.

iv. Risk Diversification: By operating multiple lines of business under one roof, universal banks can spread their risks across different activities and geographic regions. This diversification helps mitigate the impact of adverse events in any single business segment and enhances overall financial stability.

v. Economies of Scale: Universal banks can achieve economies of scale by sharing resources, infrastructure, and expertise across different business units. This can lead to cost savings and efficiency improvements, ultimately benefiting customers through lower fees and better service quality.

B. Disadvantages:

i. Conflict of Interest: Universal banks may face conflicts of interest when offering a wide range of financial services. For example, there may be conflicts between the interests of the bank's commercial banking clients and its investment banking activities, potentially leading to biased advice or unfair treatment of customers.

ii. Systemic Risk: The interconnectedness of universal banks and their involvement in multiple financial activities can contribute to systemic risk. A failure or distress in one part of the bank's operations could spill over to other areas, amplifying the impact and potentially destabilizing the entire financial system.

iii. Regulatory Complexity: Universal banking models pose regulatory challenges due to the diverse range of activities involved and the potential for regulatory arbitrage. Regulators must implement comprehensive oversight and risk management frameworks to address the unique risks associated with universal banks effectively.

iv. Information Asymmetry: Universal banks may have access to privileged information across different business lines, potentially giving them an unfair advantage over competitors or clients. This information asymmetry can undermine market integrity and erode trust in the financial system.

v. Concentration of Power: Universal banks may become too big and influential, concentrating economic and political power in the hands of a few large institutions. This concentration of power could limit competition, stifle innovation, and pose challenges to market efficiency and consumer welfare.

2.4.1. American Depository Receipts (ADRs)

American Depositary Receipts (ADRs) are financial instruments that represent ownership in shares of foreign companies traded on U.S. stock exchanges. ADRs enable investors in the United States to invest in foreign companies without needing to directly purchase shares on foreign stock exchanges or deal with foreign currency exchange. Here's how ADRs work and some key points to understand about them:

Advantages of ADR

i. Benefits for Investors: ADRs provide U.S. investors with access to international investment opportunities without the need to open foreign brokerage accounts or handle foreign currency transactions. They also offer diversification benefits by allowing investors to invest in foreign companies across different sectors and regions.

ii. Currency Risk: While ADRs are denominated in U.S. dollars, the underlying assets are foreign securities, exposing investors to currency risk. Changes in exchange rates between the U.S. dollar and the currency of the foreign company's home country can affect the value of ADRs.

iii. Tax Considerations: Investors should be aware of potential tax implications when investing in ADRs. Dividend income and capital gains from ADR investments may be subject to withholding taxes in both the United States and the foreign company's home country.

iv. Corporate Governance: ADR investors may face challenges related to corporate governance and shareholder rights, as the legal and regulatory frameworks governing corporate governance practices may differ across countries. Investors should carefully evaluate the corporate governance practices of the foreign company issuing the ADRs.

B. How ADR works

Step 1. Selection of Issuer: A foreign company, known as the issuer, decides to expand its investor base or raise capital in the U.S. market. This decision often stems from a desire to increase visibility, access liquidity in U.S. markets, or attract American investors.

Step 2. Engagement of Depositary Bank: The issuer engages a U.S.-based depositary bank to oversee the ADR program. The depositary bank serves as a bridge between the issuer, U.S. investors, and the U.S. securities market. The depositary bank ensures compliance with U.S. regulations, facilitates the issuance of ADRs, and manages ongoing ADR-related activities.

Step 3. Custody of Underlying Shares: The issuer's existing shares, known as underlying shares, are deposited with the depositary bank. These shares are typically held in custody by the depositary bank in the issuer's home country or another suitable jurisdiction.

Step 4. ADR Creation: Based on the underlying shares deposited, the depositary bank issues American Depositary Receipts (ADRs). Each ADR typically represents a specific number of underlying shares, known as the ADR-to-underlying share ratio. This ratio is determined by the depositary bank and agreed upon by the issuer.

Step 5. Listing on U.S. Stock Exchange: The ADRs are listed and traded on a U.S. stock exchange such as the New York Stock Exchange (NYSE) or Nasdaq. Listing on a U.S. exchange provides liquidity and visibility to the ADRs, making them accessible to American investors.

Step 6. Trading and Settlement: Once listed, ADRs can be bought and sold by investors on the U.S. stock exchange where they are listed. Investors can place orders through their brokerage accounts, and transactions are settled through the U.S. clearing and settlement system.

Step 7. Dividend Distribution: Dividends declared by the issuer on the underlying shares are collected by the depositary bank. The depositary bank converts these dividends into U.S. dollars and distributes them to ADR holders. Dividends can be distributed either in cash or reinvested to purchase additional ADRs, depending on the preference of the ADR holders.

Step 8. Corporate Actions: In the event of corporate actions such as stock splits, mergers, or rights offerings, the depositary bank manages the corresponding adjustments to the ADR program. The depositary bank communicates these changes to ADR holders and ensures that their rights and interests are protected.

Step 9. Custody and Redemption: ADRs are typically held in custody by the depositary bank on behalf of investors. Investors can deposit and withdraw ADRs through their brokerage accounts. In some cases, ADR holders may choose to convert their ADRs into the underlying shares, allowing them to directly own shares in the foreign company.

Step 10. Regulatory Compliance: Throughout the ADR issuance and trading process, the depositary bank ensures compliance with applicable U.S. securities laws and regulations. The depositary bank files periodic reports with the U.S. Securities and Exchange Commission (SEC) and provides transparency to investors regarding the financial condition and performance of the ADR program.

C. Disadvantages of ADR

While American Depositary Receipts (ADRs) offer numerous advantages for investors and foreign companies, they also come with some potential disadvantages. Here are several drawbacks associated with ADRs:

i. Currency Risk: ADR investors are exposed to currency risk because ADRs are denominated in U.S. dollars while the underlying shares are denominated in a foreign currency. Fluctuations in exchange rates between the U.S. dollar and the foreign currency can impact the value of ADRs, potentially leading to losses for investors.

ii. Limited Market Access: ADRs may not provide investors with direct access to the full range of securities and investment opportunities available in the foreign market. Investors may miss out on certain investment options, asset classes, or market segments that are not represented by ADRs.

iii. Regulatory and Reporting Requirements: ADR issuers are subject to regulatory and reporting requirements in both their home country and the United States. Compliance with these requirements can be complex and costly, leading to increased administrative burdens and regulatory risks for ADR issuers.

iv. Market Volatility: ADR prices may be influenced by factors such as market sentiment, geopolitical events, and regulatory changes, which can lead to increased volatility in ADR markets. Investors may experience higher levels of price fluctuations and uncertainty compared to investing in domestic securities.

v. Corporate Governance Concerns: ADR investors may face challenges related to corporate governance and shareholder rights, as legal and regulatory frameworks governing corporate governance practices may differ between the United States and the issuer's home country. Investors may have limited influence over corporate governance decisions and may face difficulties exercising their shareholder rights.

vi. Liquidity Risk: ADR liquidity may vary depending on factors such as trading volume, market demand, and investor interest. ADRs of smaller or less well-known foreign companies may have lower liquidity, making it difficult for investors to buy or sell large quantities of ADRs without significantly impacting the market price.

vii. Counterparty Risk: ADR investors are exposed to counterparty risk associated with the depositary bank that issues and administers the ADR program. If the depositary bank were to encounter financial difficulties or default, investors could face challenges accessing their ADR holdings or receiving dividends and other entitlements.

viii. Tax Complexity: ADR investors may encounter tax complexities related to dividends, capital gains, and withholding taxes. Tax treatment of ADR investments may vary depending on factors such as the investor's country of residence, the issuer's home country, and any applicable tax treaties.

2.4.2. Global Depository Receipts (GDRs)

Global Depositary Receipts (GDRs) are financial instruments that represent ownership in shares of foreign companies traded on international stock exchanges outside the company's home country. Similar to American Depositary Receipts (ADRs), GDRs facilitate cross-border investment by allowing investors to gain exposure to foreign companies without needing to directly purchase shares on foreign stock exchanges or deal with foreign currency exchange.

A. Advantages of GDR

i. Access to International Markets: GDRs provide investors with access to international investment opportunities by allowing them to invest in foreign companies listed on international stock exchanges. This enables investors to diversify their portfolios and gain exposure to companies operating in different regions and industries.

ii. Currency Risk: Like ADRs, GDRs expose investors to currency risk, as they are denominated in a currency other than the company's home currency. Fluctuations in exchange rates between the currency of the GDR and the investor's local currency can affect the value of GDR investments.

iii. Regulatory Considerations: GDRs are subject to regulatory oversight in the jurisdictions where they are listed and traded. Investors should be aware of the regulatory requirements and disclosure standards applicable to GDR issuers and consider the implications for investor protection and transparency.

iv. Tax Considerations: Investors should also consider the tax implications of investing in GDRs, including potential withholding taxes on dividend income and capital gains taxes. Tax treatment may vary depending on the investor's jurisdiction and the tax treaties in place between countries.

v. Corporate Governance: Like ADRs, GDR investors may encounter challenges related to corporate governance and shareholder rights, as legal and regulatory frameworks governing corporate governance practices may differ across countries. Investors should assess the corporate governance practices of the foreign company issuing the GDRs.

B . How GDRs Work:

Step 1. Selection of Issuer: The process begins with a foreign company (the issuer) deciding to raise capital or increase its visibility in international markets by issuing GDRs.

Step 2. Engagement of Depositary Bank: The issuer engages an international depositary bank to facilitate the GDR issuance process. The depositary bank serves as the intermediary between the issuer and investors and handles various aspects of the GDR program.

Step 3. Custody of Underlying Shares: The issuer's existing shares (underlying shares) are deposited with the depositary bank. These shares are typically held in custody by the depositary bank in the issuer's home country.

Step 4. GDR Creation: The depositary bank creates GDRs representing ownership of the underlying shares. Each GDR typically represents a specific number of underlying shares, although this ratio may vary depending on the issuing bank and the company.

Step 5. Listing on International Exchange: The depositary bank lists the GDRs on one or more international stock exchanges outside the issuer's home country. Common listing venues for GDRs include the London Stock Exchange, Luxembourg Stock Exchange, and Singapore Stock Exchange.

Step 6. Trading and Settlement: Once listed, GDRs can be bought and sold by investors on the international stock exchange where they are listed. Trading of GDRs follows the standard practices and procedures of the exchange, including order placement, execution, and settlement.

Step 7. Dividend Distribution: Dividends declared by the issuer on the underlying shares are collected by the depositary bank. The depositary bank then distributes dividends to GDR holders in accordance with the terms of the GDR program. This distribution may be in the form of cash or additional GDRs.

Step 8. Corporate Actions: In the event of corporate actions such as stock splits, mergers, or rights offerings, the depositary bank manages the corresponding adjustments to the GDR program and communicates these changes to GDR holders.

Step 9. Custody and Redemption: GDRs are typically held in custody by the depositary bank on behalf of investors. Investors can redeem their GDRs for the underlying shares held by the depositary bank, subject to the terms and conditions of the GDR program.

Step 10. Regulatory Compliance: Throughout the GDR issuance and trading process, the depositary bank ensures compliance with applicable regulatory requirements and disclosure standards in the jurisdictions where the GDRs are listed and traded.

C. Disadvantages of GDR

Global Depositary Receipts (GDRs) provide investors with exposure to foreign securities traded on international markets, but they also come with several potential disadvantages. Here are some of the drawbacks associated with GDRs:

i. Currency Risk: Similar to ADRs, GDR investors are exposed to currency risk because GDRs are denominated in a currency other than the investor's local currency. Fluctuations in exchange rates between the currency of the GDR and the investor's currency can impact the value of GDRs and result in currency-related losses.

ii. Limited Market Access: GDRs may not provide investors with direct access to the full range of securities and investment opportunities available in the foreign market. Certain investment options, asset classes, or market segments may not be represented by GDRs, limiting investors' ability to diversify their portfolios.

iii. Regulatory Compliance: GDR issuers are subject to regulatory and reporting requirements in both their home country and the jurisdiction where the GDRs are listed and traded. Compliance with these requirements can be complex and costly, leading to increased administrative burdens and regulatory risks for GDR issuers.

iv. Market Volatility: GDR prices may be influenced by factors such as market sentiment, geopolitical events, and regulatory changes, which can lead to increased volatility in GDR markets. Investors may experience higher levels of price fluctuations and uncertainty compared to investing in domestic securities.

v. Corporate Governance Concerns: GDR investors may face challenges related to corporate governance and shareholder rights, as legal and regulatory frameworks governing corporate governance practices may differ between jurisdictions. Investors may have limited influence over corporate governance decisions and may face difficulties exercising their shareholder rights.

vi. Liquidity Risk: GDR liquidity may vary depending on factors such as trading volume, market demand, and investor interest. GDRs of smaller or less well-known foreign companies may have lower liquidity, making it difficult for investors to buy or sell large quantities of GDRs without significantly impacting the market price.

vii. Counterparty Risk: GDR investors are exposed to counterparty risk associated with the depositary bank that issues and administers the GDR program. If the depositary bank were to encounter financial difficulties or default, investors could face challenges accessing their GDR holdings or receiving dividends and other entitlements.

viii. Tax Complexity: GDR investors may encounter tax complexities related to dividends, capital gains, and withholding taxes. Tax treatment of GDR investments may vary depending on factors such as the investor's country of residence, the issuer's home country, and any applicable tax treaties.

2.5 EXIM Bank

The Export-Import Bank of India (EXIM Bank) is a specialized financial institution established in 1982 under the Export-Import Bank of India Act, 1981. It is wholly owned by the Government of India and was created to promote Indian exports and facilitate cross-border trade and investment. EXIM Bank provides a range of financial services, including loans, guarantees, and advisory services, to Indian exporters and importers. The bank plays a pivotal role in enhancing the competitiveness of Indian businesses in the global market.

EXIM Bank's mission is to enhance India's competitiveness in the global marketplace, promote Indian exports, and facilitate international trade and investment. It aims to support Indian businesses, particularly exporters, by providing them with financial assistance, advisory services, and risk management solutions.

A. Functions of EXIM Bank

The Export-Import Bank, often referred to as EXIM Bank, plays a crucial role in facilitating international trade and supporting economic development. Here are the key functions typically associated with EXIM Banks:

i. Export Financing: EXIM Banks provide financial assistance to exporters in the form of loans, lines of credit, and guarantees to support their export activities. This financing helps exporters fulfill orders, expand production capacity, and enter new markets.

ii. Import Financing: EXIM Banks offer financing solutions to importers, including import loans, letters of credit, and trade finance facilities. Import financing helps importers secure the necessary funds to purchase goods and services from overseas suppliers.

iii. Export Credit Insurance: EXIM Banks provide export credit insurance to protect exporters against the risk of non-payment by foreign buyers. This insurance coverage helps exporters mitigate credit risk, safeguard their cash flow, and enhance their ability to offer competitive credit terms to buyers.

iv. Project Finance: EXIM Banks support large-scale infrastructure projects and international investments through project finance solutions. They provide financing, guarantees, and advisory services to facilitate the development and implementation of projects in sectors such as energy, transportation, telecommunications, and manufacturing.

v. Trade Promotion: EXIM Banks promote international trade and investment by organizing trade missions, participating in trade fairs and exhibitions, and providing market intelligence and advisory services to exporters and importers. They help businesses identify export opportunities, access new markets, and navigate trade barriers.

vi. Policy Advocacy: EXIM Banks advocate for policies and regulations that facilitate trade and investment, reduce trade barriers, and promote economic growth. They work closely with government agencies, industry associations, and international organizations to address trade-related challenges and promote a favorable business environment for exporters and importers.

vii. Capacity Building: EXIM Banks offer training programs, workshops, and educational resources to build the capacity of exporters, importers, and other stakeholders involved in international trade. These capacity-building initiatives help businesses improve their export readiness, enhance their trade finance skills, and comply with international trade regulations.

viii. Risk Management: EXIM Banks help businesses manage various risks associated with international trade, including credit risk, currency risk, political risk, and market risk. They offer risk mitigation tools such as credit guarantees, export credit insurance, and hedging instruments to protect businesses against potential losses.

B. Impact of EXIM Bank

The Export-Import Bank of India (EXIM Bank) wields significant influence on the nation's economy, exerting its impact across various sectors and dimensions. By fervently promoting Indian exports, EXIM Bank serves as a cornerstone for businesses, offering vital financial assistance, credit insurance, and advisory services to exporters. This bolstering facilitates access to global markets, enabling exporters to fulfill orders, compete robustly, and enrich India's foreign exchange reserves while engendering employment opportunities. Moreover, the bank's focused support for Small and Medium Enterprises (SMEs) galvanizes the backbone of India's export sector, nurturing competitiveness and fostering growth within these vital economic contributors. Simultaneously, EXIM Bank propels infrastructure development endeavors through its provision of long-term financing, guarantees, and advisory services. This aids in the realization of critical projects, spanning transportation, power generation, and telecommunications, thus fueling economic growth and amplifying India's connectivity with global markets. Additionally, by facilitating Indian companies' overseas investments, EXIM Bank spearheads a wave of international expansion, fortifying India's global presence and fostering cross-border economic cooperation. Its relentless advocacy for policies conducive to trade growth, coupled with its role in promoting market diversification, further underscores its paramount importance in sculpting India's economic landscape, cementing its position as a catalyst for inclusive and sustainable development.

Key aspects take away from Unit 2

2.1. Meaning of Central Bank

- **Definition**: A central bank is a national institution that manages a country's currency, money supply, and interest rates.
- **Key Roles**: It oversees monetary policy, regulates financial institutions, acts as a lender of last resort, and maintains financial stability.

2.2. History of Reserve Bank of India

- **Establishment**: Founded on April 1, 1935, under the Reserve Bank of India Act, 1934.
- **Milestones**: Nationalized in 1949; significant reforms in the 1990s liberalization era.
- **Evolution**: Has evolved from a purely monetary authority to a multi-faceted entity influencing the broader financial sector.

2.3. Functions of Reserve Bank of India

- **Monetary Authority**: Formulates and implements monetary policy to maintain price stability and ensure adequate flow of credit.
- **Regulator and Supervisor**: Oversees and regulates the banking sector to ensure its health and stability.
- **Issuer of Currency**: Sole authority to issue currency notes in India.
- **Developmental Role**: Supports various economic sectors through specific programs and policies.
- **Financial Inclusion**: Initiatives to ensure the financial inclusion of underserved sectors.

- **Foreign Exchange Management**: Manages the Foreign Exchange Management Act, 1999 and ensures smooth functioning of the foreign exchange market.

2.4. Universal Banking System

- **Definition**: A system where banks offer a wide variety of financial services, including commercial and investment banking.
- **Scope**: Banks provide loans, savings, investment services, insurance, and more under one roof.

2.4.1. American Depository Receipts (ADR)

Advantages:

- Access to American markets for non-U.S. companies.
- Diversification for investors.
- Enhanced visibility and prestige for issuing companies.

Functioning: ADRs are traded on American stock exchanges, representing shares in a foreign company.

Disadvantages:

- Costs of compliance with U.S. regulations.
- Currency risk and exchange rate fluctuations.

2.4.2. Global Depository Receipts (GDR)

Advantages:

- Access to multiple international markets.
- Broader investor base and increased capital inflow.
- Improved corporate image and visibility.

Functioning: GDRs are traded on international stock exchanges, representing shares in a foreign company.

Disadvantages:

- Regulatory and compliance costs.
- Exchange rate and currency risks.
- Market accessibility may be limited compared to local listings.

2.5. EXIM Bank

- **Role**: Export-Import Bank of India (EXIM Bank) provides financial assistance to promote Indian exports and facilitate cross-border trade and investment.
- **Functions**: Offers export credit, financing, guarantees, advisory services, and promotes international partnerships.

2.6.1. Functions of EXIM Bank

- **Credit Facilities**: Provides pre-shipment and post-shipment credit.
- **Overseas Investment Finance**: Supports Indian firms in overseas acquisitions and joint ventures.
- **Guarantees and Insurance**: Mitigates risks for exporters through credit guarantees and insurance.

Advisory Services: Offers market advisory services and capacity-building programs.

2.6.2. Impact on Indian Economy

- **Trade Growth**: Facilitates an increase in Indian exports by providing financial products and services.
- **Economic Development**: Promotes industrial growth and technological advancements through support for exports.

- **Global Presence**: Helps Indian companies establish a presence in international markets, enhancing global trade connections.
- **Financial Stability**: Mitigates export risks, contributing to overall economic stability and growth.

Check Your Progress

Exercise

A. Answer the following in brief. (Short Notes)

1. What is the meaning of a Central Bank?
2. Can you provide a brief history of the Reserve Bank of India?
3. What are the key functions of the Reserve Bank of India?
4. What is a Universal Banking System?
5. Can you explain the concept of American Depository Receipts (ADR) in terms of its advantages, functioning, and disadvantages?
6. How do Global Depository Receipts (GDR) work and what are their advantages and disadvantages?
7. What is the role of EXIM Bank?
8. What are the functions of EXIM Bank?
9. How does EXIM Bank impact the Indian economy?

B. Answer the following in detail. (Long answer type question)

1. Explain the concept of a central bank and its role within a nation's financial system. Discuss the key functions of a central bank, including monetary policy, bank regulation, and government banking. How does a central bank influence economic stability and growth?
2. Trace the historical development of the Reserve Bank of India (RBI). Discuss the factors that led to the establishment of the RBI and its evolving role over the years. How has the RBI's function adapted to the changing economic landscape of India?
3. Elaborate on the various functions of the Reserve Bank of

India. Discuss its role as the monetary authority, regulator of the banking system, manager of foreign exchange reserves, and banker to the government. How do these functions contribute to achieving the RBI's objectives?

4. Define the concept of a universal banking system and compare it to traditional banking models. Discuss the advantages and disadvantages of a universal banking system for both institutions and consumers. Analyze the impact of a universal banking system on financial inclusion and economic development.
5. Explain the concept of American Depositary Receipts (ADRs) and their role in facilitating international investment. Discuss the advantages and disadvantages of using ADRs for foreign companies seeking to raise capital in the US market. How does the issuance and trading of ADRs impact foreign exchange markets and global investment strategies?
6. Elaborate on the specific advantages of using ADRs for foreign companies, such as increased access to US investors, improved liquidity, and brand recognition.
7. Explain the process of issuing and trading ADRs, including the role of depository banks and the underlying foreign securities. Discuss the different types of ADRs and their respective features.
8. Analyze the potential drawbacks of using ADRs, such as currency exchange fluctuations, additional regulatory costs, and potential for lower investor returns.
9. Compare and contrast Global Depositary Receipts (GDRs) with American Depositary Receipts (ADRs). Discuss the key differences in terms of target markets, regulatory requirements, and potential benefits for issuing companies. When might a company choose a GDR over an ADR?
10. Explain the specific advantages of using GDRs for foreign

companies, such as access to a broader pool of international investors and potential for higher fundraising capacity.

11. Describe the process of issuing and trading GDRs, highlighting the similarities and differences compared to ADRs. Discuss the role of depository banks and the underlying foreign securities.
12. Analyze the potential drawbacks of using GDRs, such as potentially higher listing costs, complex regulatory environments, and lower market liquidity compared to established markets.
13. Explain the role and functions of the Export-Import Bank of India (EXIM Bank) in promoting India's foreign trade. Discuss the various financial instruments used by EXIM Bank to support Indian exporters and importers. How does EXIM Bank contribute to India's economic growth and international trade competitiveness?
14. Elaborate on the specific functions of EXIM Bank, such as providing pre-shipment and post-shipment credit, guaranteeing export receivables, and offering lines of credit to foreign buyers. Analyze how these functions address the financial needs of Indian businesses engaged in international trade.
15. Discuss the positive and negative impacts of EXIM Bank's activities on the Indian economy. Analyze how EXIM Bank's role in promoting exports and foreign trade contributes to economic growth, job creation, and foreign exchange reserves. Additionally, consider potential drawbacks, such as the risk of bad debt or overdependence on certain export markets.

Chapter 03

Fundamentals of Insurance

3.1. Definitions of Banks

Insurance is a financial arrangement between an individual or entity (the insured) and an insurance company (the insurer), where the insured pays a premium in exchange for the insurer's promise to compensate for specific potential future losses. This arrangement helps individuals and businesses protect themselves against financial loss from unforeseen events such as accidents, natural disasters, illness, and death. Insurance works on the principle of risk pooling, where many policyholders' premiums are pooled together to cover the losses of a few. This collective risk-sharing mechanism provides financial stability and security to policyholders.

3.2 Purpose and Need of Insurance

Insurance serves multiple purposes and fulfills various needs for individuals, businesses, and society.

i. Risk Management: Insurance helps individuals and businesses manage various risks by transferring the financial burden of potential losses to an insurance company. It provides protection against unexpected events such as accidents, illnesses, natural disasters, and other unforeseen circumstances.

ii. Financial Protection: Insurance offers financial protection to individuals and businesses by providing compensation or coverage for losses or damages. This protection can include medical expenses, property damage, liability claims, and more, depending on the type of insurance policy.

iii. Peace of Mind: Having insurance coverage provides peace of mind to individuals and businesses, knowing that they are protected against financial losses resulting from covered events. This sense of security allows people to focus on their daily lives and business operations without constantly worrying about potential risks.

iv. Legal Requirements: In many cases, insurance is a legal requirement. For example, auto insurance is mandatory in most countries to cover liability in case of accidents. Similarly, businesses may be required to have certain types of insurance coverage to comply with regulatory requirements.

v. Business Continuity: Insurance helps businesses maintain continuity by providing financial support in the event of unexpected losses or disruptions. With the right insurance coverage, businesses can recover more quickly from setbacks and continue their operations without significant financial strain.

vi. Investment Protection: Insurance also serves as a tool for protecting investments. For example, property insurance protects real estate investments, while life insurance provides financial support to beneficiaries in the event of the policyholder's death, safeguarding their financial future.

vii. Social Welfare: Insurance contributes to social welfare by spreading the financial risks across a larger pool of policyholders. This pooling of risks helps reduce the financial burden on individuals and businesses when they experience losses, fostering economic stability and resilience.

viii. Encouraging Responsible Behavior: Insurance companies often incentivize policyholders to adopt safer practices and behaviors by offering discounts or lower premiums for measures that reduce the likelihood of claims. This encourages individuals and businesses to take proactive steps to mitigate risks, ultimately benefiting society.

3.3 Significance of Insurance

Insurance is significant for several reasons, impacting individuals, businesses, and the broader economy:

i. Protection Against Uncertainty: Insurance provides protection against unforeseen events, offering peace of mind and financial stability. This allows individuals and businesses to plan with confidence.

ii. Encouraging Savings: Insurance policies, particularly life insurance, encourage savings and financial planning. Policyholders pay regular premiums, which can accumulate and provide returns, contributing to long-term financial goals.

iii. Promoting Investment: By mitigating risk, insurance encourages investment in businesses, infrastructure, and personal ventures. Investors and entrepreneurs are more willing to take calculated risks knowing they have insurance coverage.

iv. Supporting Economic Growth: Insurance contributes to economic growth by mobilizing savings and directing them into productive investments. Insurance companies invest premiums in various financial instruments, supporting economic development.

v. Enhancing Creditworthiness: Insurance enhances creditworthiness by providing lenders with the assurance that their loans are protected. For example, mortgage insurance ensures that lenders are protected in case the borrower defaults.

3.4 Principles of Insurance

The principles of insurance form the foundation upon which insurance contracts and policies are built. These principles guide the insurance industry in its operations and interactions with policyholders. Here are the key principles of insurance:

i. Utmost Good Faith (Uberrimae Fidei): This principle requires both the insurer and the insured to act with the utmost good faith and honesty in all their dealings. It implies full disclosure of all material facts relevant to the insurance contract. Any deliberate withholding or misrepresentation of information can invalidate the contract.

ii. Insurable Interest: Insurable interest means that the insured must have a financial stake or interest in the subject matter of the insurance policy. In other words, the insured must suffer a financial loss if the insured event occurs. This principle ensures that insurance contracts are not speculative, and that the insured has a legitimate reason to seek coverage.

iii. Indemnity: The principle of indemnity states that the purpose of insurance is to restore the insured to the same financial position they were in before the loss occurred, without allowing for profit. In other words, insurance compensates for the actual financial loss suffered, up to the policy limit, but does not allow the insured to profit from the loss.

iv. Proximate Cause: This principle determines the cause of loss or damage that is covered by the insurance policy. The insurer will assess the proximate or nearest cause of the loss to determine whether it falls within the scope of coverage. Events directly caused by covered perils are typically covered, while those caused by excluded perils may not be covered.

v. Subrogation: Subrogation is the right of the insurer to step into the shoes of the insured after settling a claim and pursue legal remedies against third parties responsible for the loss. This principle prevents the insured from collecting double recovery for the same loss and helps insurers mitigate their losses by recovering funds from responsible parties.

vi. Contribution: Contribution applies when multiple insurance policies cover the same risk or property. Each insurer shares the cost of the claim proportionally based on the coverage provided by their policy. This principle prevents overcompensation and ensures that no insurer pays more than its fair share of the claim.

vii. Mitigation of Loss: Insured parties have a duty to take reasonable steps to minimize the extent of their losses after an insured event occurs. Failing to mitigate losses could affect the insurer's liability under the policy. This principle encourages insured parties to act responsibly to limit the financial impact of covered events.

3.5 Types of Insurance

Insurance can be broadly classified into two main categories: life insurance and general insurance. Each category encompasses various types of insurance policies tailored to meet specific needs.

3.5.1 Life Insurance

Life insurance provides financial protection against the risk of death. It ensures that the beneficiaries receive a lump sum payment upon the policyholder's death, helping to secure their financial future.

i. Term Life Insurance: Term life insurance provides coverage for a specified period, typically ranging from 5 to 30 years. If the insured individual dies within the term of the policy, the insurer pays out a death benefit to the designated beneficiaries. Term life insurance is typically more affordable than permanent life insurance and is suitable for individuals' seeking coverage for a specific time period, such as to replace lost income during their working years or to cover a mortgage.

ii. Whole Life Insurance: Whole life insurance provides coverage for the entire lifetime of the insured, as long as premiums are paid. It offers a death benefit to beneficiaries and also includes a cash value component that grows over time. The cash value accumulates on a tax-deferred basis and can be accessed by the policyholder through withdrawals or loans. Whole life insurance provides lifelong coverage and can serve as a tool for wealth accumulation and estate planning.

iii. Universal Life Insurance: Universal life insurance is a flexible permanent life insurance policy that allows policyholders to adjust their premium payments and death benefits over time. It consists of a death benefit, cash value component, and a separate account where premiums are invested. Policyholders can increase or decrease the death benefit and vary premium payments within certain limits, providing flexibility to adapt to changing financial circumstances.

iv. Variable Life Insurance: Variable life insurance combines a death benefit with an investment component, allowing policyholders to allocate premiums to various investment options such as stocks, bonds, and mutual funds. The cash value of the policy fluctuates based on the performance of the underlying investments, offering the potential for higher returns but also bearing investment risk. Variable life insurance provides flexibility and potential growth but requires active management of investment choices.

v. Indexed Universal Life Insurance: Indexed universal life insurance is a type of universal life insurance that offers a death benefit and a cash value component linked to the performance of a stock market index, such as the S&P 500. Policyholders can participate in market gains up to a certain cap while being protected from market downturns with a minimum guaranteed interest rate. Indexed universal life insurance combines the flexibility of universal life with the potential for higher returns based on market performance.

vi. Final Expense Insurance: Final expense insurance, also known as burial insurance or funeral insurance, is a type of whole life insurance designed to cover end-of-life expenses such as funeral costs, medical bills, and other debts. It typically offers smaller death benefits compared to traditional life insurance policies and is suitable for individuals who want to ensure their loved ones are not burdened with funeral expenses.

3.5.2 General Insurance

In India, several types of general insurance are popular due to the diverse risks faced by individuals, businesses, and assets. Here are some of the most popular types of general insurance in India:

A. Motor Insurance:

i. Motor Vehicle Insurance: Compulsory Third-Party Liability Insurance is mandatory for all vehicles in India under the Motor Vehicles

Act. Comprehensive insurance covering own damage is also widely popular, providing coverage for damages to the insured vehicle due to accidents, theft, fire, or natural disasters.

A. **Health Insurance**:

i. Mediclaim Insurance: Health insurance policies cover medical expenses, hospitalization costs, and sometimes additional benefits such as pre- and post-hospitalization expenses, ambulance charges, and critical illness coverage.

ii. Family Floater Health Insurance: Provides coverage for the entire family under a single policy, offering financial protection against medical emergencies for all family members.

iii. Personal Accident Insurance: Offers coverage for accidental death, disability, or injury resulting from accidents, providing financial support to the insured and their family.

A. **Home Insurance**:

i. Homeowners Insurance: Covers damages to the structure of the home, as well as personal belongings, against perils such as fire, theft, burglary, natural disasters, and more.

ii. Rural Insurance: Tailored insurance products for rural dwellings, agricultural structures, and rural assets, providing protection against specific risks prevalent in rural areas.

A. **Travel Insurance**:

i. Travel Health Insurance: Provides coverage for medical expenses, emergency medical evacuation, trip cancellation, baggage loss, and other travel-related risks during domestic and international travel.

ii. Student Travel Insurance: Designed for students studying abroad, offering coverage for medical emergencies, study interruptions, and other travel-related risks.

E. Crop Insurance:

i. Pradhan Mantri Fasal Bima Yojana (PMFBY): Government-sponsored crop insurance scheme aimed at providing financial support to farmers in case of crop loss due to natural calamities, pests, or diseases.

ii. Weather-Based Crop Insurance: Provides coverage against adverse weather conditions that affect crop yields, such as drought, excess rainfall, or temperature fluctuations.

F. Commercial Insurance:

i. Fire Insurance: Protects commercial properties, factories, warehouses, and business premises against fire and allied perils.

ii. Marine Cargo Insurance: Covers goods in transit by sea, air, or land against loss or damage during transportation.

iii. Liability Insurance: Provides coverage for third-party liability claims arising from business operations, including public liability, product liability, and professional liability.

G. Miscellaneous Insurance:

i. Burglary Insurance: Covers loss or damage to insured property due to burglary, theft, or housebreaking.

ii. Terrorism Insurance: Offers coverage against damages or losses resulting from terrorist activities, including property damage, business interruption, and liability claims.

3.6 Risks Associated with Insurance

Managing these risks requires insurance companies to implement robust risk management practices, diversify their portfolios, maintain adequate capital reserves, and stay vigilant to changes in the regulatory and business environment. Additionally, effective communication, transparency, and ethical conduct are essential for maintaining trust and credibility with stakeholders. The risks associated with insurance:

i. Underwriting Risk: Insurance companies face the risk of underwriting policies for individuals or businesses that may incur higher-than-expected losses. Inadequate underwriting assessments can lead to financial losses if claims exceed premiums collected.

ii. Moral Hazard: Moral hazard occurs when insured individuals or businesses alter their behavior after obtaining insurance coverage, leading to increased risks or losses. For example, individuals may engage in riskier behavior if they believe their insurance will cover any resulting damages.

iii. Adverse Selection: Adverse selection refers to the tendency for individuals with higher-than-average risks to seek insurance coverage, while lower-risk individuals may choose not to insure themselves. This imbalance can lead to higher claim ratios and increased costs for insurers.

iv. Catastrophic Risk: Insurance companies face the risk of catastrophic events such as natural disasters, pandemics, or large-scale accidents that result in a high volume of claims and significant financial losses. Catastrophic events can strain insurers' financial resources and solvency.

v. Investment Risk: Insurers invest premiums collected from policyholders to generate returns and cover future claim payments. However, investment risks, such as market volatility, credit risk, and interest rate fluctuations, can affect the performance of investment portfolios and ultimately impact insurers' financial stability.

vi. Regulatory Risk: Insurance companies operate within a regulatory framework governed by laws, regulations, and supervisory authorities. Changes in regulations, compliance requirements, or government policies can introduce uncertainty and impact insurers' operations, profitability, and competitive landscape.

vii. Reputation Risk: Insurers face reputation risk if they fail to meet policyholder expectations, provide inadequate customer service, or experience negative publicity due to claims disputes, financial instability, or unethical behavior. Damage to reputation can lead to loss of trust, customer attrition, and diminished market competitiveness.

viii. Operational Risk: Operational risks include internal factors such as system failures, fraud, human errors, or disruptions in business operations. Insurers must implement robust risk management practices and controls to mitigate operational risks and safeguard their operations and reputation.

ix. Liquidity Risk: Insurance companies need sufficient liquidity to meet their obligations, including claim payments, policyholder withdrawals, and operating expenses. Liquidity risk arises when insurers face difficulties in accessing liquid assets or obtaining additional funding during periods of financial stress.

x. Litigation Risk: Insurers are exposed to litigation risk from policyholders, beneficiaries, or third parties who may file lawsuits alleging breach of contract, negligence, or other legal claims. Legal expenses and settlements associated with litigation can impact insurers' financial performance and profitability.

3.7 Regulatory Body of Insurance

The insurance industry is regulated by government authorities to ensure its integrity, stability, and protection of policyholders' interests. In India, the primary regulatory body for insurance is the Insurance Regulatory and Development Authority of India (IRDAI).

In India, the regulatory body overseeing the insurance sector is the Insurance Regulatory and Development Authority of India (IRDAI). Established in 1999 under the Insurance Regulatory and Development Authority Act, 1999, IRDAI is responsible for regulating and promoting the insurance industry in the country.

Role of IRDAI

The Insurance Regulatory and Development Authority of India (IRDAI) plays a pivotal role in regulating and promoting the insurance sector in India. Here are some key roles and functions of IRDAI:

i. Regulatory Oversight: IRDAI regulates and supervises insurance companies, intermediaries, and related entities operating in India. It ensures compliance with applicable laws, regulations, and guidelines to maintain the integrity, stability, and efficiency of the insurance market.

ii. Licensing and Registration: IRDAI grants licenses and registrations to insurance companies, agents, brokers, surveyors, and other intermediaries involved in the insurance business. It establishes eligibility criteria and evaluates applications to ensure that only qualified entities operate in the sector.

iii. Consumer Protection: IRDAI works to protect the interests of policyholders and consumers by enforcing fair treatment, transparency, and integrity in insurance products, sales, and services. It addresses consumer grievances, resolves disputes, and promotes consumer awareness and education.

iv. Market Development: IRDAI promotes the development and growth of the insurance market by formulating policies, guidelines, and initiatives to enhance market competitiveness, innovation, and penetration. It encourages the introduction of new products, distribution channels, and technology-driven solutions to meet evolving consumer needs.

v. Financial Stability and Solvency: IRDAI monitors the financial condition and solvency of insurance companies to ensure their ability to meet policyholder obligations and withstand adverse events. It establishes prudential norms, capital requirements, and risk management standards to maintain financial stability and protect policyholder interests.

vi. Market Conduct Regulation: IRDAI regulates market conduct practices and compliance with regulatory requirements by insurance companies and intermediaries. It promotes ethical business conduct, fair competition, and adherence to professional standards to maintain market integrity and consumer trust.

vii. Policy Formulation and Research: IRDAI formulates policies, conducts research, and provides recommendations on various aspects of insurance regulation, market development, risk management, and emerging trends. It collaborates with stakeholders to address industry challenges, promote innovation, and facilitate sustainable growth.

viii. International Collaboration: IRDAI engages in international cooperation and collaboration with regulatory bodies and organizations worldwide. It participates in forums, exchanges information, and adopts best practices to enhance regulatory effectiveness, align with global standards, and foster cross-border cooperation.

Key aspects take away from Unit 3

3.1. Definition of Insurance

Insurance: A financial arrangement providing protection against potential future losses or risks by transferring the risk from an individual or entity to an insurance company in exchange for premiums.

3.2. Purpose and Need of Insurance

Purpose:

- Risk Management: Provides financial protection against unexpected events.
- Financial Stability: Helps individuals and businesses recover from losses.
- Social Security: Offers a safety net for individuals and families.

Need:

- Mitigates financial impact of risks such as accidents, illnesses, and natural disasters.
- Encourages savings and investment by reducing uncertainty.
- Essential for economic stability and growth by protecting assets and investments.

3.3. Significance of Insurance

- **Economic Growth**: Supports economic development by enabling risk-taking and investment.
- **Social Welfare**: Reduces the financial burden on individuals and families during crises.
- **Financial Security**: Ensures continuity of business operations after losses.
- **Resource Allocation**: Promotes optimal allocation of resources by reducing the need for emergency funds.

3.4. Principles of Insurance

- **Utmost Good Faith**: Both parties (insurer and insured) must disclose all relevant information honestly.
- **Insurable Interest**: The insured must have a legitimate interest in the subject matter of insurance.
- **Indemnity**: Insurance aims to restore the insured to their original financial position before the loss.
- **Contribution**: Multiple insurers covering the same risk will share the loss proportionally.
- **Subrogation**: The insurer can take over the insured's rights to recover from a third party responsible for the loss.
- **Proximate Cause**: The primary cause of loss must be covered by the policy for the claim to be valid.

3.5. Types of Insurance

3.5.1. Life Insurance

Definition: Provides financial protection against the loss of life. Benefits are paid to beneficiaries upon the insured's death.

Types:

- Term Life Insurance: Provides coverage for a specific period.
- Whole Life Insurance: Offers lifetime coverage with a savings component.

- Endowment Plans: Combines life coverage with savings for a specific term.
- Unit-Linked Insurance Plans (ULIPs): Combines investment and insurance.

3.5.2. General Insurance

- **Definition**: Provides protection against non-life risks such as property damage, liability, and health issues.

Types:

- Health Insurance: Covers medical expenses.
- Motor Insurance: Covers vehicles against accidents, theft, and third-party liability.
- Property Insurance: Protects property against risks like fire, theft, and natural disasters.
- Travel Insurance: Covers risks associated with travel, such as trip cancellations and medical emergencies abroad.
- Liability Insurance: Protects against legal liabilities due to damages caused to third parties.

3.6. Risks Associated with Insurance

- **Underwriting Risk**: Risk of underwriting losses due to incorrect risk assessment.
- **Market Risk**: Potential financial loss due to market fluctuations affecting investments.
- **Credit Risk**: Risk of default by counterparties, affecting the insurer's ability to pay claims.
- **Operational Risk**: Risks arising from internal processes, systems failures, or human errors.
- **Liquidity Risk**: Risk of being unable to meet short-term

financial obligations.

- **Regulatory Risk**: Changes in laws and regulations that can affect the insurer's operations and profitability.

3.7. Regulatory Body of Insurance

- **In India**: The Insurance Regulatory and Development Authority of India (IRDAI)

Functions:

- Regulates and supervises the insurance industry.
- Protects policyholders' interests.
- Ensures financial soundness of insurance companies.
- Promotes the development of the insurance sector.
- Enforces compliance with statutory regulations.
- Monitors and resolves consumer grievances.

Check Your Progress

Exercise

A. Answer the following in brief. (Short Notes)

1. What is the definition of insurance?
2. Why do individuals and businesses need insurance?
3. How does insurance help mitigate financial risks?
4. What is the significance of insurance in modern society?
5. Why is insurance important for businesses and individuals?
6. What are the fundamental principles of insurance?
7. Explain the principle of utmost good faith in insurance.
8. How does the principle of indemnity apply in insurance contracts?
9. What are the main types of insurance?
10. Provide examples of different types of insurance policies.
11. What is life insurance, and how does it differ from other types of insurance?
12. What are the primary purposes of life insurance?
13. What is general insurance, and what types of risks does it cover?
14. How does general insurance contribute to risk management for businesses?
15. How do insurers manage underwriting risk?
16. What are the main functions of the regulatory body in insurance?
17. How does the regulatory body protect the interests of policyholders?

B. Answer the following in detail. (Long answer type question)

1. Explain the concept of pooling of risks and how insurance spreads the financial impact of losses among a larger group of policyholders.
2. Discuss the multifaceted purposes and needs that insurance fulfills for individuals, businesses, and society as a whole.
3. How does insurance address the fundamental human need for financial security and stability, particularly in the face of unforeseen events and risks?
4. Analyze the significance of insurance in promoting economic stability, resilience, and social welfare, particularly in the context of risk management and financial protection.
5. Explore in detail the fundamental principles that govern insurance contracts, including utmost good faith, insurable interest, indemnity, and others.
6. How do these principles ensure fairness, transparency, and efficiency in insurance transactions, balancing the interests of insurers and policyholders?
7. Provide examples illustrating how insurance principles are applied in practice, shaping the terms and conditions of insurance policies and claims settlement processes.
8. Provide a comprehensive overview of the main types of insurance, categorizing them into life insurance and general insurance, and exploring their respective features and functions.
9. Identify and analyze the various risks inherent in the insurance industry, including underwriting risk, moral hazard, adverse selection, and others.
10. How do insurers manage and mitigate these risks through underwriting practices, risk assessment tools, and diversification strategies?
11. Explain the role and functions of the regulatory body responsible for overseeing the insurance sector, such as the

Insurance Regulatory and Development Authority of India (IRDAI).

12. How does the regulatory body ensure compliance with applicable laws, regulations, and prudential norms, safeguarding the interests of policyholders and promoting market integrity?

###

About Author

Surjeet Kumar: A Life Dedicated to Learning and Inspiring Others

Surjeet Kumar's life is a testament to the boundless power of dedication and passion. Having embarked on his teaching career immediately upon completing high school, he has carved a path that transcends conventional expectations. His unwavering commitment to education has not only nurtured countless young minds but has also fueled his own intellectual growth. Kumar's dedication to his students extends far beyond the classroom. He has diligently pursued postgraduate studies, continually enriching his knowledge and expertise. Moreover, he has authored a series of textbooks, including *Principles of Finance* , *Business Ethics* , *Basics of Corporate Accounting* , *Fundamentals of Banking and Insurance* , and many more, sharing his invaluable insights with a wider audience.

While excelling in academia, Kumar has not neglected his artistic pursuits. His soul finds solace and expression in poetry. He has authored several collections of poems, including *Peculiar Version of Primitive Proverbs (in two volumes), Silence the Louder Scream , and Embers Ignited Fury Unbound, Shor Khamoshi ka, Bayar Veerah Ki, Goonjti Gustakhiyan, Pallav Prem Ke.* These books likely touch upon the vast experiences gleaned from his dual roles as an educator and learner.

Kumar's journey continues to be marked by remarkable achievements. The recent release of his textbooks signifies his unwavering commitment to sharing his accumulated knowledge and insights with a wider audience, impacting countless lives beyond the confines of his classrooms.

www.ingramcontent.com/pod-product-compliance
Lightning Source LLC
LaVergne TN
LVHW090427210926
848480LV00002B/718
9798231529681